MEN
Shining With Youthful
BRILLIANCE

*Guidance to the Men
of the SGI–USA*

DAISAKU IKEDA

World Tribune
Press

Santa Monica, California

Contents

Foreword

To the members of the SGI-USA men's division who are shining as the golden pillars of global *kosen-rufu*:

Thanks to you, our SGI-USA has made remarkable development as an outstanding organization of peace, culture and education that is giving unlimited hope to the world.

I deeply appreciate the constant, strenuous efforts of my dearest men's division members of the SGI-USA to support the great women's division and protect the pure youth division, as you simultaneously expand the circle of trust and security. I, too, am a member of the honored men's division.

The SGI-USA has made another new departure with its three-territory organizational system. I am truly delighted that the men's division has commenced its own further advancement under the leadership of three of my trusted and youthful leaders in the respective territories with John Kasahara in the East Territory, James Herrmann in the Central Territory and Steve Mortan in the West Territory.

Sixty years have passed since I first met my mentor, Josei Toda. In the midst of the harsh conditions of the Japanese economy following World War II, I fought like an *asura* demon to protect my mentor while upholding his business enterprises.

In those days, I deeply etched in my life passages from Hall Caine's *The Eternal City* that I studied under my mentor's guidance. Caine wrote that people can become their strongest through suffering and forbearance (see Hall Caine, *The Eternal City*; New York: D. Appleton and Company, 1901, p. 67). One character calls out to the people of Rome, "Be brave, be strong, be patient, and tomorrow night you will send up such a cry as will ring throughout the world" (p. 281).

Kosen-rufu does not exist somewhere in the distance. It is found in your steady, day-to-day accumulation of victories over your own challenging issues in your family, in your career and in your community. *Kosen-rufu* means the ceaseless, noble battle of human revolution to expand the challenge of self-reformation in your community, in your society and in the entire world.

Shijo Kingo, a predecessor of the men's division, endured false accusations from his colleagues and groundless persecutions from his lord simply because he persisted in his faith in Nichiren Daishonin's Buddhism.

He also had to face real-life problems such as the serious illness of his infant daughter. Engraving deep in his life all the encouragement that he received from Nichiren Daishonin, he overcame every difficulty, showing superb actual proof of victory through his courageous faith.

Nichiren Daishonin wrote to encourage Shijo Kingo: "Kyo'o's misfortune will change into fortune. Muster your faith, and pray to this Gohonzon. Then what is there that cannot be achieved?" (*The Writings of Nichiren Daishonin*, vol. 1, p. 412) and "Nam-myoho-renge-kyo is like the roar of a lion. What sickness can therefore be an obstacle?" (WND-1, 412).

As long as you persevere with profound prayer and courageous action, you can make every obstacle a source of growth, changing each into a cause for your happiness. Nothing is impossible with this faith.

I hope that my men's division members will open up a new golden era of the SGI-USA with profound conviction and the brave heart of a lion king. Many ranks of young people are following in your footsteps.

I hope that you will strive patiently, steadfastly and resolutely to build an unshakable "golden castle of capable people" while cherishing the youth as if they were your own sons and daughters or your own brothers and sisters.

Expressing his great expectations for the SGI, Dr. M. S. Swaminathan, a world-renowned scholar in the field of agriculture and a fighter for peace and humanism who has published a dialogue with me, has said: "The time has come for the human revolution, the alternative to which is human extinction. We must now examine in great depth the important question of social and cultural reformations, originating with the human revolution."

Proud members of the SGI-USA men's division! You are standing at the forefront of the second act of global *kosen-rufu* whose shining curtain has just been raised. Please send waves of joy and victory from the United States to Japan and the entire world! I will dedicate my life more than ever to the development of American *kosen-rufu*.

I conclude my foreword here with the prayer that this book of collected guidance for the men's division will become a source of nourishment in faith for my men's division members and a source of energy for further progress.

Cheers for August 24, Men's Division Day! Cheers to the SGI-USA!

DAISAKU IKEDA
August 2007

The Men's Division Begins

The following excerpt is from The New Human Revolution, *vol. 10, "Crown Champions" chapter, pp. 315–25, which is set in 1966.*

March 5 was a beautiful, clear spring day in Tokyo. Shin'ichi Yamamoto looked forward to this day with great anticipation. In the evening, a ceremony marking the establishment of the men's division, which had been announced at the February 27 Headquarters Leaders Meeting, would be held at the Soka Gakkai Headquarters. During the day, whenever Shin'ichi saw one of the Headquarters staff who would be joining the new division, he would joyfully remark: "The time for men of the Soka Gakkai to stand up is here at last. The curtain will now rise on an age of full-fledged activities for *kosen-rufu*."

Shin'ichi firmly believed that the members of the men's division were the pillars supporting the grand structure of *kosen-rufu*. During the time of Nichiren Daishonin, it was his middle-aged male disciples who played central roles among the laity.

For example, Shijo Kingo, one of the Daishonin's leading disciples in Kamakura, was about forty years old when he accompanied the Daishonin during the Tatsunokuchi Persecution, prepared to give his own life to protect his mentor. It was also from his mid-forties that he tried to persuade his lord Ema to take faith in the Daishonin's Buddhism and bravely endured personal attacks and persecution that arose as a result, including the confiscation of some of his lands.

Despite this, Shijo Kingo is often thought of as a youthful follower of the Daishonin. This impression is partly due to the fact that he was twenty-seven when he began practicing. More than anything, however, it can be attributed to his single-minded devotion to *kosen-rufu*, his sincerity and his incredible passion.

The Japanese name for the men's division is *sonen-bu*—with *bu* meaning "division" and *sonen* literally meaning "men in the prime of life." It is important therefore that the men's division members, while on the one hand being self-possessed and level-headed, also demonstrate courage, energy and action as people who burn with a passionate commitment to *kosen-rufu*.

In addition to Shijo Kingo in Kamakura, the core followers of the Daishonin in the Shimosa region were Toki Jonin, Ota Jomyo and Soya Kyoshin, all men in their prime.

Toki Jonin gave the Daishonin refuge in his own home following the Matsubagayatsu Persecution, where Pure Land school believers made an attempt on the Daishonin's life. Several years the Daishonin's senior, he joined in the struggle to spread the Mystic Law when he was in his mid-forties. Ota Jomyo, who was introduced to the Daishonin's teachings by Toki Jonin, is thought to have been around the same age as the Daishonin. Soya

Kyoshin was two years younger than Jomyo. Thus, at the time of the Tatsunokuchi Persecution in 1271, Toki Jonin was around fifty-six years old, Ota Jomyo was about fifty and Soya Kyoshin was about forty-eight.

Because these men rose up to valiantly strive and encouraged their fellow practitioners to do the same, they served as pillars of strength for many followers, who were inspired to persevere in faith amid great persecution.

Where there are such men, others feel reassured. When men stand up, it gives others courage. Their presence is significant and their potential is tremendous.

At five o'clock in the afternoon, the ceremony marking the establishment of the men's division began in the hall on the third floor of the Soka Gakkai Headquarters. The brilliant rays of the setting sun poured into the room.

Shin'ichi led everyone in a solemn *gongyo* [reciting portions of the Lotus Sutra and chanting Nam-myoho-renge-kyo]. The participants' faces shone with joy, excited to think that the time had come for them to demonstrate their real abilities. Shin'ichi prayed wholeheartedly that the members of the men's division, the great bulwark of the Soka Gakkai, would resolutely stand up.

Afterwards, General Director Izumida addressed the gathering. He encouraged the participants to win in their workplaces and make outstanding contributions to their communities, gaining trust in society at large. Shin'ichi sat forward in his seat and applauded.

Men in their prime hold many key leadership positions in society. An important factor, therefore, in realizing a peaceful society based on Buddhist ideals lies in the men's division members playing active roles in every area of society and developing into great leaders.

The age of the essential phase of *kosen-rufu* is the time when each individual manifests actual proof of their practice based on the principle of faith equals daily life.

The general director's remarks were followed by greetings from the vice leaders of the new division and then guidance from President Yamamoto.

Shin'ichi smiled broadly and said: "Congratulations on the establishment of the men's division. I am truly overjoyed that this day has come and I feel even more confident about the future of *kosen-rufu*."

This was Shin'ichi's honest sentiment. Next he stated that for the sake of the continuous advancement of *kosen-rufu*, it was important to combine the strength of conservative caution with the youthful, vigorous spirit of reform, adding that it had been the exemplary efforts of maturity and youth together that had contributed to the Soka Gakkai's progress thus far. He further remarked that at this time of new beginning in the organization's movement, both the power of youth that fuels *kosen-rufu*'s development and the experience and wisdom of the mature, well-rounded men's members were crucial.

Shin'ichi then touched upon the role of the men's division within the Soka Gakkai as a whole: "It goes without saying that our organization advances through the cooperation of its various divisions. However, just as fathers are often the backbone of their families, the members of the men's division have an important mission to ensure the success of our activities. That is why men serve as central figures in each chapter and district.

"While one of the men's division's main functions is to foster men, I hope you will not view yourselves as just one of the Gakkai's divisions but that you will promote harmony among all and shoulder responsibility for protecting the Soka Gakkai and the entire membership."

Shouts of affirmation and applause filled the room.

Shin'ichi said: "If the men's division sets an outstanding example, then the women's, young men's and young women's divisions will also splendidly develop. The sincere encouragement of the men's division will help to nurture truly capable people in every division.

"I would particularly like you to support the young men as they strive to reveal their potential, providing them with opportunities to actively work on the front lines and taking full responsibility for their development. I would also like you to warmly support and protect the women's and young women's members. The men's division is a model of faith for the other divisions. Everyone is watching to see how all of you, with the wide range of practical life experience you possess, will tackle your various challenges.

"If you persevere with strong faith no matter what happens, members of the other divisions will readily follow your admirable example. If, on the other hand, you are insincere and shrewdly maneuver circumstances to your own benefit, behave halfheartedly or abandon your faith, it will cause others to lose sight of their goals and perhaps even to doubt their faith. Indeed, the role of the men's division is significant."

Shin'ichi wanted to impress upon them the importance of carrying out faith throughout their lives. It is not uncommon to see men's passion wane as they get older, even though they may have been vigorously active in their youth and vowed to devote themselves to *kosen-rufu*. There are many reasons for this. One is that they become busier in their jobs as a result of increased responsibility; sometimes illness or declining health is the cause. There are other instances in which they allow their faith to lapse, feeling that because they have given so much energy to their Soka Gakkai activities in the past, they deserve a break.

Of course, there are times in one's life when work must take top priority. Also, when one falls ill, it is important to rest and recuperate. But Buddhist practice is something we pursue throughout our life. No matter what circumstances we may encounter, it is vital that we never regress in faith. Even the slightest inclination to do so means that our faith is slipping, even though we may not be aware of it.

Nichiren Daishonin writes: "Strengthen your faith day by day and month after month. Should you slacken in your resolve even a bit, devils will take advantage" (WND-1, 997). If we backslide in faith or fall victim to negligence or cowardice even a little, we create an opening by which the devilish functions can enter to try to destroy our faith and the foundation of our happiness.

It was Shin'ichi's hope that all the members of the men's division would dedicate themselves to pursuing the path of attaining Buddhahood in this lifetime, to achieving their human revolution and to realizing glory and victory across the three existences. To abandon faith is to betray oneself. Pointing to the pitiful end that had come to those members who had left the Soka Gakkai and slandered and attacked President Toda and the organization, he spoke to the men about the importance of carrying out faith throughout their lives.

His voice rang with the firm determination not to allow even a single member to fall by the wayside: "No one can escape the strict workings of the Buddhist law of cause and effect. That's why, no matter how you are denounced or criticized, it is vital that you remain steadfast in faith, always believing in the Gohonzon and sticking with the Soka Gakkai, certain of the great inconspicuous benefit you are accumulating.

"Quoting the Lotus Sutra, the Daishonin clearly states that those who uphold strong faith 'will enjoy peace and security in their present existence and good circumstances in future existences' (LS5, 99). There is no falsity in the words of Nichiren Daishonin."

Shin'ichi's voice grew more forceful: "You, the members of the men's division, are entering a period of securing the foundation for the final chapter of your lives. Each of you possess great ability. I hope you will apply all of your talents to the advancement of *kosen-rufu*.

"The Daishonin writes: 'Since death is the same in either case, you should be willing to offer your life for the Lotus Sutra. Think of this offering as a drop of dew rejoining the ocean, or a speck of dust returning to the earth' (WND-1, 1003). Because none of us can escape death, the Daishonin urges us to give our lives for the sake of the Lotus Sutra, the eternal Law of life. In other words, he tells us to use our lives working for *kosen-rufu*.

"That is the only way to become one with the Mystic Law, the great life of the universe, and to live an eternal life, just as a dew drop rejoins the ocean and a speck of dust returns to the earth. A lifetime passes quickly. And the period in that lifetime when we can be energetic and active is limited. Once people reach middle age, it all seems to go by in an instant.

"If you don't stand up now, when will you? If you don't exert yourselves now, when will you? How many decades do you intend to wait before you take your stand? There is no telling what condition you will be in then. You are in the prime of your life. It is a precious time in this present finite existence. I say this because I want you to have no regrets!"

Shin'ichi's voice, reverberating like the roar of a lion, deeply struck the hearts of the men.

The participants listened earnestly, wanting to absorb every word. He continued: "President Makiguchi took faith when he was fifty-seven years old. President Toda was forty-five when he stood up alone to carry out *kosen-rufu* following his release from prison. They were both around the same age as many of you when they aroused great faith and embarked on the challenge of advancing *kosen-rufu*. This is a Soka Gakkai tradition.

"I am also a member of the men's division. I hope that you will join me and rise up valiantly with the Gakkai spirit and become golden pillars supporting the citadel of Soka."

The members' faces shone with the determination of champions of *kosen-rufu*.

In closing, Shin'ichi said: "I am counting on you. If the men's division develops remarkably and establishes a solid framework for *kosen-rufu*, our organization will remain secure forever."

Thunderous applause, infused with the members' proud and joyous vow to carry out *kosen-rufu*, reverberated endlessly throughout the room.

Next, Kazumasa Morikawa, one of the new general administrators, read the editorial that Shin'ichi had just completed for the April edition of *The Daibyakurenge* study journal, titled "Valiant Champions of the Mystic Law." In it, Shin'ichi set forth the attributes of such people.

The first was absolute conviction in the power of the Gohonzon; second, the ability to face and challenge difficulties; third, to be a leader well versed in all matters of society; fourth, passion to foster younger members; fifth, to be a broad-minded and humanistic leader; and sixth, a strong sense of duty and the ability to draw up a plan of action.

Approximately six years had passed since Shin'ichi had become president of the Soka Gakkai. Now, preparations for a new phase of *kosen-rufu* were complete.

Shin'ichi bowed to the participants and made way to leave the room. Then he stopped, raised his fist and called out: "Everyone! Let's strive together! Let's make a history of fresh achievements! If we are going to live this life, let us use it striving dynamically for the sake of the Law!"

The members raised their fists in response and shouted out in agreement. Tears shone in many an eye. Their hearts burned with fighting spirit. Filled with pride, these crown champions, great warriors of the Mystic Law, began their gallant march into the future.

Outside, the sky had grown dark, but the third floor of the Soka Gakkai Headquarters blazed with the light of joy.

MESSAGE

Buddhism Concerns Itself With Victory or Defeat

JUNE 16, 2007

TO MY BELOVED MEMBERS of the men's division of Los Angeles! I send my sincere congratulations on the holding of your general meeting that heralds a new era in American *kosen-rufu*. I truly appreciate your efforts to gather for this meeting even though this is a holiday weekend when most people are taking a rest.

I feel that I am attending this gathering of courageous men together with you as a member of the men's division.

A succession of changes characterizes society and the times in which we are living. I am certain that you are struggling with the hardships that naturally arise in the course of life. So long as you keep faith in the core of your lives, all the struggles and sufferings you are going through will ultimately dignify your lives, creating limitless fortune and virtue. With a great sense of purpose in your mission for the propagation of Buddhism, you can contribute to the happiness of your beloved families and precious friends.

Life is a stage for either winning or losing. Victory or defeat also matters in society. Buddhism concerns itself with victory or defeat. Even in the midst of the grave persecution of his exile to Sado, Nichiren Daishonin persisted in his victorious advancement without retreating even a step, stating, "It has been twenty or more years now since I found myself in that situation and began the great battle. Not once have I thought of retreat" (WND-2, 464).

I hope that you, the members of the men's division, as the golden pillars of *kosen-rufu*, will carry out dauntless faith throughout your lives to ensure absolute victory based upon the oneness of mentor and disciple.

Let's fight together for American *kosen-rufu*, a driving force for global *kosen-rufu*, with a disciplined, strong life force.

You are all so very important to me. From the bottom of my heart, I am praying for your good health and happiness. Please convey my warmest regards to your family members.

DAISAKU IKEDA, SGI PRESIDENT

Prayer Is the Source of Victory

JANUARY 27, 2007

MY CHERISHED LEADERS of the SGI-USA men's division! My sincere congratulations on holding your executive conference.

In Tokyo, I am watching your dedication with my utmost admiration for your spirited struggles. You are showing splendid actual proof in gaining trust from your respective communities while standing out as shining and indispensable models in society.

Buddhism is concerned with winning. Your human revolution lies in your ceaseless endeavors to establish victory after victory. A victorious existence means you are carrying out your human revolution in the most honorable way.

Every aspect of life is a battle. So is our pursuit of *kosen-rufu*. Only when you actually win can you prove that your cause has been just and true.

Never retreat under any circumstances. Live an undefeated existence. Even if you are temporarily defeated, aim to win the next challenge dauntlessly, proclaiming, "This defeat will bring about future victory." If you are defeated today, all you have to do is to win tomorrow.

Nichiren Daishonin writes, "When with our mouths we chant the Mystic Law, our Buddha nature, being summoned, will invariably emerge" (WND-1, 887). Through chanting Nam-myoho-renge-kyo as rhythmically as a galloping white horse and through your resonant voices, please call forth the Buddha's life from within, letting the brilliant sun of the eternal aspect of your life—your enlightened nature—rise in your heart. Prayer is the source of victory. Prayer is the driving force to fight.

The SGI-USA men's division, trailblazers of American kosen-rufu! Win continuously with optimism by employing the "strategy of the Lotus Sutra." With this said, I conclude my message. Please take excellent leadership in your individual locale. Fight together with me, always in good health.

Please convey my warmest regards to your family and the people in your respective communities.

DAISAKU IKEDA, SGI PRESIDENT

The Golden Pillar of American Kosen-rufu

September 22, 2006

To my most respected and trusted members of the men's division of the SGI-USA! Thank you so much for your constant efforts!

I wish I could fly to the Florida Nature and Culture Center, converse with you, and sing together with all my heart. With my most sincere cheers to you, I am overseeing all your activities at the FNCC.

My men's division of the SGI-USA is a golden pillar of American *kosen-rufu*. Your courageous struggles are a precious, major driving force for the advancement of *kosen-rufu* in America. Your wisdom and experience will enable us to gain trust from American society without fail. Your existence will serve as a cornerstone in our challenge to be trusted in the community.

Showing an exemplary way of living with robust faith is your mission as a member of the men's division. Nichiren Daishonin states, "The purpose of the appearance in this world of Shakyamuni Buddha, the lord of teachings, lies in his behavior as a human being" (WND-1, 852). The greatness of faith is reflected in the way you live your life. In other words, it will be manifested in the action you take.

The beloved members of the men's division! Please win a most victorious and superbly happy existence while devoting yourselves as proud Bodhisattvas of the Earth to fight the evil that hinders the progress of *kosen-rufu*.

Furthermore, please embrace the women's and young women's divisions with all your broad-mindedness. Please exert yourselves strongly to foster the youth division. Please advance in the unity of "many in body but one in mind" in a manner that is most harmonious and exemplary for the whole world.

I am earnestly chanting Nam-myoho-renge-kyo for you in hopes that you, without a single exception, will emerge victorious in your tough battle amid the severe realities of society and forge on along the glorious path of total contentment.

Please convey my warmest regards to your families and friends.

DAISAKU IKEDA, SGI PRESIDENT

Men Shining With Youthful Brilliance

AUGUST 2005

Every August, the SGI-USA men's division members hold meetings to commemorate August 24, 1947, the day SGI President Daisaku Ikeda joined the Soka Gakkai, and to celebrate the unique role the men's division members play as pillars of their families, society and the SGI-USA.

MY DEAR, NOBLE MEMBERS of the SGI-USA men's division! My heartfelt congratulations to you for holding your general meeting. I thank all of the members, their friends and guests who have gathered today despite busy schedules, and I also thank those who worked hard behind the scenes to prepare for the success of this meeting.

The SGI-USA men's division is truly the pillar of the organization and the mainstay of our *kosen-rufu* movement. You are spearheading the expansion of *kosen-rufu* in your respective communities. As a men's division member, I am fully aware of how hard it is, while struggling amid the tough realities of society, to carry out a dynamic battle day and night for your friends' happiness and for the sake of *kosen-rufu*. For that, you have my deepest respect.

When Shijo Kingo, a samurai believer who today would be an exemplary member of the men's division, was deeply troubled, Nichiren Daishonin encouraged him, writing, "Live so that all the people of Kamakura will say in your praise that Nakatsukasa Saburo Saemon-no-jo [also known as Shijo Kingo] is diligent in the service of his lord, in the service of Buddhism, and in his concern for other people" (WND-1, 851).

This passage can be taken as the Daishonin's guidance to us that no matter how trying our circumstances, we should never give up and that we should gain the trust of those around us while becoming leading figures in our individual fields. In other words, through this passage, the Daishonin encourages us to play a key role in spreading the Mystic Law as humanistic leaders upon whom fellow comrades can rely. This passage is an eternal guideline for the men's division.

Please confront all hardships with composure and resolute faith and show splendid actual proof of victory. A creative, dauntless and youthful life will enable you to shine forth brilliantly with great benefit and virtue. When you live in such a manner, you are certainly contributing to your family's eternal happiness and prosperity.

Today, America is taking on an increasingly significant role in our movement. I will support America now more than ever. Members of the men's division, please become important cornerstones for the great advancement of the SGI-USA in the spirit of "many in body, one in mind." I hope you will function as a driving force in opening a new phase of American *kosen-rufu*. I am praying wholeheartedly every day for your good health, happiness and long life. I hope each of you will achieve one breakthrough after another, while making today's general meeting the greatest, most enjoyable and most meaningful.

Cheers to the men of the SGI-USA!

DAISAKU IKEDA, SGI PRESIDENT

(Originally published in the August 19, 2005, World Tribune, *p. 1)*

ESSAY

Live With Honor

THE NINETEENTH-CENTURY English poet Anne Brontë wrote, *"While Faith is with me, I am blest; / It turns my darkest night to day."* We are living out our lives with faith in the supreme Mystic Law. It is the magnificent Buddhism of the sun, which enables us to overcome every obstacle and hardship, to triumph over whatever destiny may bring. Never forget that it sets human beings on the truest, most powerful and profoundest orbit of victory in life. As men's division members, it is our honorable mission and duty to resolutely protect this noble realm of faith, a realm of integrity and happiness, from any and all devilish forces and to impart boundless dignity and strength to all our fellow members.

The renowned British historian Arnold J. Toynbee endured a turbulent life. He witnessed two world wars in which many friends from his university days fell in battle. He also suffered the loss of a beloved son. He was assailed by baseless slander, and he experienced life's difficulties in full measure. Nonetheless, Toynbee stayed strong, living up to his credo to exert himself on behalf of others.

Even in his eighties, he awoke each morning at 6:45 and, after breakfast, started working by 9:00. No matter how he felt that day, he sat down at his desk and set to the task at hand. As he once said to me, "If you wait until you feel like working, you'll never accomplish anything." To the last days of his life, he courageously and steadfastly remained shoulder to the wheel, struggling to accomplish all he could, embodying his perennial motto—*Laboremus* (Let's get to work).

Let us, too, get to work again today, take on new challenges, set out in our respective places of mission. Let us launch into the great struggle for *kosen-rufu*. Nichiren Daishonin writes: "Life is limited; we must not begrudge it. What we should ultimately aspire to is the Buddha land" (WND-1, 214). Brave and tenacious individuals of firm resolve are certain to win out in the end, no matter how arduous the challenge.

Euripides, the eminent poet and playwright of ancient Greece, asked rhetorically: "Can any man attain great honors without effort? Has ever a weak and lazy man obtained the highest prize?" Of course not. On June 7, 2005, the maritime adventurer Ken'ichi Horie returned home safely to Japan after completing a nonstop solo circumnavigation of the globe in a sailboat following an eastward route. I have counted Mr. Horie as a dear friend for more than a decade.

When he crossed the equator on his latest voyage, I sent him a message: "Stay vigilant. Victory will be yours. My best wishes for your successful voyage." I also had a message conveyed to him just before he sailed around Cape Horn at the southern tip of South America, the most perilous part of the journey, "I'm looking forward to the safe return of the world's greatest hero." When I learned of his triumphant homecoming, I gave a shout of delight.

This was Mr. Horie's third voyage around the world. Now that he has also sailed the eastward route, he has become only the second person in history to have made such a nonstop solo circumnavigation in both eastward and westward directions. Mr. Horie is sixty-six. His latest voyage took 250 days and covered some 31,069 miles. Why does he continue challenging himself in this way?

"Once you've savored the sublime experience of surpassing your personal limits," he says, "you can't help but want to do it again."

What a youthful spirit, what invincible courage. He is indeed a champion of champions. He first crossed the Pacific when he was twenty-three. Since then, he has embarked on many adventurous voyages. He has often sailed into rough seas. Sometimes his sailboat has toppled over or even flipped upside down. But he has learned from each experience. Instead of being cowed by his failures, he regards them as lessons and makes them the fuel for future success.

As he has said, "New abilities can be drawn forth by continually challenging oneself and making efforts."

Life is like a sea voyage. We each need to open up our own course in life with the strength of our convictions, unperturbed by the crashing breakers of life's stormy seas. The fiercer the tempest rages, the more we need to rouse our own fighting spirit and man the tiller with all our strength and skill, crying, "Bring it on!" Through this type of arduous struggle, we can forge the practical wisdom to triumph consistently and, as victorious champions, create history.

The realities of society are quite strict. The world can be a cruel and harsh place. Though economic conditions may be improving, society's front lines remain a turbulent scene of desperate struggle.

It is sheer agony to suffer a business failure. I was forced to experience this myself when working for my mentor, Josei Toda, helping with his businesses. It became a lesson ingrained in me. I will never forget the haggard look on Mr. Toda's usually unruffled countenance.

It was a moment of true crisis for him. As a young man, I made a life-or-death effort to support him. He couldn't pay me. My fellow workers quit. I was in terrible health. Yet, in spite of all that, I fought like a demon to protect Mr. Toda. And from the most desperate of straits, through the combined efforts of mentor and disciple dedicated to *kosen-rufu*, we overcame every hardship, clearing the way to Mr. Toda's inauguration in 1951 as the second Soka Gakkai president.

He was fifty-one—at the height of his abilities. He declared: "All

I care about is *kosen-rufu*. Here I will make my stand. I am not afraid of anything anyone might say. There's nothing that can stop me."

Buddhism is primarily concerned with winning. The purpose of Buddhism and faith is to enable us to do just that. Mentor and disciple dedicated to *kosen-rufu* share the sublime mission to resolutely demonstrate their faith through achieving absolute victory in life and society.

One of the epithets of a Buddha is "Hero of the World." A Buddha is a valiant and noble champion who has conquered the sufferings of life in the real world.

The Daishonin writes: "Buddhism is like the body, and society like the shadow. When the body bends, so does the shadow" (WND-1, 1039). People cannot live apart from society. But to be constantly at the mercy of society's ups and downs is a miserable existence. It is crucial for us to be strong and wise. The "body" the Daishonin refers to is, on the personal level, our faith. Come what may, we need to summon our faith, hold our heads up and bravely face the challenges before us. No matter how difficult the situation seems, decide that you will beat it and chant with all your might. This is the all-powerful and invincible strategy of the Lotus Sutra.

Men's division members are staunch leaders who guide our troubled and tumultuous world in a positive direction. The German poet Friedrich Hölderlin wrote that all great undertakings are a battle that can only be won through strength and spirit. My praiseworthy fellow men's division members, since fight we must, let us fight joyously and courageously for a great cause. And, for the sake of the young people who will come after us, let us triumph over every obstacle with indomitable strength and spirit, for faith is our highest right, which we have freely chosen.

The Daishonin wrote a letter to the father of Nanjo Tokimitsu. Though the father had converted to the Daishonin's teachings, he remained confused and could not completely give up his attachment to his former erroneous beliefs. Hence, in this letter, the Daishonin admonishes him not to be "of two minds" or "fear what others may say" (WND-1, 82). To be "of two minds" here indicates a state of doubt and weakness in which one cannot commit oneself wholeheartedly to faith in the Lotus Sutra.

Genuine faith means to single-mindedly carry out one's belief. On the other hand, timidly fearing what others will think, unable to refute opponents of the Lotus Sutra, is to be "of two minds." Those of two minds can never attain Buddhahood, no matter how deeply they study the Buddhist teachings. To know what is correct and what is mistaken and yet neglect to speak up when the time comes is, in the Daishonin's stern words, to act as a "deadly enemy of all living beings" who is "bound to fall into the great citadel of the Avichi hell" (WND-1, 607).

Leaving it up to others to promote *kosen-rufu* is, in a strict sense, just another form of being "of two minds." Also, the Daishonin states, "To hope to attain Buddhahood without speaking out against slander is as futile as trying to find water in the midst of fire or fire in the midst of water" (WND-1, 747). In the end, halfhearted efforts only result in an eternity of regrets. This is self-defeating. It is important to commit yourself. Charge ahead, without hesitation, and live out your life carrying the banner of the Soka movement as a proud member of the Soka Gakkai men's division.

Nichiren Daishonin proclaims: "The essential message in this work ['The Opening of the Eyes'] is that the destiny of Japan depends solely upon Nichiren. A house without pillars collapses, and a person without a soul is dead. Nichiren is the soul of the people of this country" (WND-1, 772). The Soka Gakkai, which has inherited the spirit of establishing the correct teaching for the peace of the land, is the pillar and soul of Japan. And the men's division serves as the central pillar of the Soka Gakkai, a great bastion of noble ordinary people.

"It is better to live a single day with honor than to live to 120 and die in disgrace," declares the Daishonin (WND-1, 851). A day dedicated to *kosen-rufu* is a precious day of good fortune that will last forever. Please do not leave yourself with regrets. The Scottish poet Robert Burns wrote, *"Now's the day, and now's the hour; / See the front o' battle lour [threaten]."* Now is the time to stand up and face the challenge. No matter what happens, never retreat; battle on to the very end.

The secret to victory in any struggle is fervent prayer. The next step is boldly to take action. Maintaining courage, hope and perseverance, let us inspire everyone to action and encourage one another toward victory. This is the formula for winning in any endeavor. To the young men's division members, to the praiseworthy active retirees who make up the *Taiyo-kai* and to all the members of the men's division, the wonderful golden pillar of kosen-rufu: Do not be defeated. My valiant men's division champions—let's fight together and score triumph after triumph.

This essay was published in the "Light of the Century of Humanity" series in the July 2, 2005, Seikyo Shimbun, *the Soka Gakkai's daily newspaper. It subsequently appeared in the September 23, 2005,* World Tribune, *p. 2.*

The Great Champions of Kosen-rufu

AUGUST 24, 2004

To ALL OF YOU, the golden pillars of worldwide *kosen-rufu*, the men's division members of the SGI-USA for whom I have the greatest respect and admiration: Congratulations on the occasion of this profoundly significant men's division general meeting. Thank you for your constant sincere efforts for the sake of your families, fellow members and society.

I have only the highest praise for you, knowing of the valiant efforts you have made in spite of your busy schedules to attend this general meeting. There is no doubt that the Buddhas and bodhisattvas throughout the ten directions and three existences are lauding your noble seeking spirit and your dedicated commitment to kosen-rufu, while the innumerable positive forces of the universe are rigorously protecting each one of you. In light of the teachings of the Lotus Sutra and Nichiren Daishonin, your steadfast faith will endow your families and loved ones with immense good fortune without fail.

Nichiren Daishonin writes: "'Great vow' refers to the propagation of the Lotus Sutra" (OTT, 82). The SGI, dedicated to carrying out the Buddha's intent and decree, has inherited this great vow in exact accord with the spirit of Shakyamuni and Nichiren Daishonin and resolutely advanced the movement for *kosen-rufu* in the world today. As the solid, reliable pillars of the SGI, you, the members of the men's division, are working tirelessly to contribute to the prosperity of your communities and countries as well as the happiness and welfare of others. The eternal honor and merit you are gaining through these selfless efforts are immeasurable. I hope that you will always maintain this conviction and pride, making your way with courage and hope while leading lives of resounding victory.

In a letter to Shijo Kingo, who could be called a predecessor of today's men's division, the Daishonin writes: "It is better to live a single day with honor" (WND-1, 851). "With honor" means being an honorable, admirable person and boldly carrying out our great mission and responsibilities so that we have no regrets. It is to strive courageously to do our best each day, no matter what others may say, no matter what our circumstances may be. It is to continuously advance on the path of "faith equals daily life" and "Buddhism manifests itself in society" and create a brilliant history of achievement. This is the noble life that all of you, great champions of *kosen-rufu*, are leading.

In another of his writings, the Daishonin states: "A person of considerable strength, when alone, may fall down on an uneven path. . . . Therefore, the best way to attain Buddhahood is to encounter a good friend" (WND-1, 598). Without the existence of a good organization and staunch comrades united in the cause of *kosen-rufu*, it is difficult to progress unerringly on the correct path of faith. The SGI is the organization of *kosen-rufu*, and it exists to enable each of its members without exception to attain lives of unsurpassed happiness and fulfillment.

I hope that you, the members of the men's division, will play a pivotal role in that effort. May you advance exuberantly in a spirit of unity and friendship, warmly encouraging and supporting one another along the way. May you also staunchly support the members of the women's and youth divisions. Please demonstrate confident leadership based on courageous faith and shining wisdom.

In closing, I offer my sincere prayers for your excellent health and long life and for the happiness and prosperity of your families. Please convey my best regards to your family and fellow members. Three cheers for the SGI-USA men's division!

DAISAKU IKEDA, SGI PRESIDENT

Men of Dedication and Commitment

I AM NOT OBLIGED to fall into decline. I am not obliged to be miserable. I have a right to be happy. The honest and true have a right to triumph.

I despise the arrogant. Irrespective of their status or celebrity, they will remain strangers to a genuinely fulfilling life.

I love people who sincerely work on their continuing growth and development. How sublime it is to look up at the heavens and converse with the stars after a discussion meeting—on cold winter nights, on sweltering summer nights, on cool spring and autumn nights. I have won again today. I have savored life's essence.

Seeing those controlled by earthly desires succumb to the countless vices that plague society and be tossed about by fate, I know with confidence that I stand on the victory tower of the greatest possible life. Though people may call me a nobody, though I may be slandered and maligned, though others may plot and scheme against me, through my powerful, overflowing prayers, I stand with dignity as an undaunted victor.

How wretched are the smug. How pathetic the avaricious and dark-hearted. How horrible is the appearance of the fearful demons whose all-consuming jealousy drives them to seek others' downfall. In the words of Leo Tolstoy, "You can neither weigh nor measure the harm done by false faith." No matter how such malevolent forces may try to torment or harass us—good, upright ordinary people—having discovered my life's indestructibility, I am filled to the very core of my being with supreme happiness.

My life shines with an eternally youthful spirit. This fresh, vibrant spirit, brimming with great, burgeoning energy, conquers the future's uncertainty.

Sufferings are an inescapable part of our lives, which are subject to the absolute rule of birth, aging, sickness and death. Worldly honors and riches all fade eventually, and the smirks of the mighty will be forever extinguished without a trace. They are destined to wander in darkness, a realm of gloom and lifeless dust.

But we have that magnificent moment of life that is prayer. A boundless horizon of hope and victory unfolds before me as I look to the future. I have no fear. Leading my life with a deep and solemn conviction, I fear nothing. I pursue life's highest course by embracing faith in the Mystic Law. There, the fresh winds of victory blow, and the banner of triumph and happiness flies proudly.

Today again, I will turn back defeat. For the sake of all, I will live out each day as a champion of good health. Life is to be lived with joy, not spent in sadness and sorrow. I do not live to suffer but to accomplish a grand purpose, embraced in solid, enduring happiness.

Even now, I vividly recall my father and how much I looked up to him when I was a child.

We lived next door to my uncle, my father's younger brother. A cherry tree and a field planted with vegetables stood in front of our houses. Beyond them lay a large, deep pond filled with carp and other fish. In the evening, birds would gather there—a beautiful sight. One day, while quite small, I was running after dragonflies when I accidentally fell into the pond. As I remember, our house was about 200 or 250 feet away. A playmate ran to my house for help. My father rushed to the pond, his face ashen.

Seeing me flailing in the water, he scooped me up in his big arms and rescued me. He was so strong, it was like being lifted by a giant crane. I clung to him desperately. The warmth of his body, that sensation, that strength, the entire scene—nearly seventy years have passed, but I will never forget it.

Another time, in the fall of the year I was in the fifth grade, I think it was, a typhoon hit our house in the middle of the night. High winds ripped tiles and iron sheeting from the roof and smashed several windows, sending shards of glass flying into the rooms. Wind gusted in through the openings and carried away the mosquito nets hanging over our beds. In the pitch-black house, my other siblings and I were all terrified. Our three older brothers had already been drafted by then and sent off to war. My father called out: "Don't worry! There's no need to be afraid! Father's here, so don't worry. Just go back to sleep." I was so impressed by his confident voice, his dauntless attitude at that time of crisis. I can still hear my father's words today.

There is no formula for grading fathers, ranking this one over that one. No matter his social status, a father is a father. Fatherhood itself is a mark of greatness.

It is wrong to inflict pain and sorrow on others. It is good and right to put people's minds at ease, to lead them to peace and happiness. This is how the great live their lives.

My friends, do not give up and hurtle down the path of despair. Do not lead such foolish, miserable lives. Win over yourselves. As fathers, be determined to carry out a father's duty and warmly embrace and protect all. As fathers, you have an important mission to provide happiness and security for your families and, through your examples, to silently teach the profound path of life. This will also become your own treasure.

Should you fall ill, you can still bring laughter and joy to your loved ones. Should you be poor and lack worldly goods, be cheerful and upbeat and make your family laugh as hard as if you were a famous comedian. Proclaim brightly, "We aren't wealthy because we've given everything for *kosen-rufu*." (Sometimes you have to stretch the truth a little!)

You may not have material wealth, but you have an imperishable treasure in the form of spiritual riches. A wise man once said: "Where there is no fortune to fight over, there are no sibling squabbles. This is compassion."

A mother declared to her children: "I have nothing to leave you. That's also compassion." From times of old, outstanding men and women have often come from poor families.

A clever young child once observed: "On Mother's Day, everyone happily gives their mom a heartfelt present, but they pay hardly any attention to their dad on Father's Day. There's even worldwide debate about why we have a Father's Day."

There are all kinds of fathers. Some sleep late and some are early risers; some are always ranting and raving, while others are kind and gentle; some skip their sutra recitation, and others actively introduce Buddhism to others. But they have one thing in common: they are all fathers. In honor of Father's Day, allow me to express my sincerest gratitude to all the fathers of *kosen-rufu* striving alongside me.

In some families, a daughter might exclaim: "Dad! You're going to ruin your eyesight watching so much television." If his wife said the same thing, he would snap back at her to mind her own business. But when his daughter says it, he listens (to the extent that he turns the volume down and goes right on watching!).

One day, the wife gives him a sound scolding. How pitiful he looks! Who would believe that he's the president of a major company or the top leader of a large organization or a university professor or a noted politician or an accomplished diplomat?

His daughter is the family's expert on everything, and her father is little more than her assistant. A man's position in society means nothing at home. True happiness is found in the ties of the heart.

A father comes home in a very bad mood. Perhaps his boss raked him over the coals. An ill-timed remark from his wife can set off a volley of angry words that, though they stop short of an all-out war, will certainly create a nasty firestorm.

Whenever he behaves arrogantly, or on the rare occasion when he vents his frustrations on his family, he inevitably loses and soon finds himself apologizing profusely to his wife. He might say to his daughter, possibly through tears: "Let's be good to Mom."

How wise is a father who always bears in mind the Sakha proverb, "It is easy to destroy but hard to create."

The daughter, in turn, might implore her parents: "Can't you just stop your silly arguing? Quarreling with each other is such a waste of time!" Perhaps, she'll urge her father: "Let's really show Mom our appreciation and get along as a happy family."

"You're right, you're right. It's my fault," the father says, his standard response.

"Can't you think of something more original to say?" the daughter exclaims, exasperated. If you challenge your own negativity, you won't get caught up in meaningless arguments.

Otherwise, even when you think you've won, you haven't really. Your family will get the better of you, ultimately. Nevertheless, the father heroically goes out and wins in society.

One father, who was normally gruff and fearless, like a much-decorated military man, wept until his tears ran dry when his beloved daughter announced she was getting married. Mother and daughter whispered to each other: "Is he sad or happy?" The closer the wedding day approached, the more despondent he became, until he seemed ready to expire. They observed his deep emotion, but they knew he'd be fine, saying: "After all, he has correct faith."

A daughter impishly asks her father, whom she knows is good on Buddhist theory but thin on practice: "My dear father, what in your opinion is the most important thing in creating a happy family?"

He responds with all seriousness: "Well, as the Daishonin writes: 'It is the heart that is important' (WND-1, 1000). What matters is whether your heart is in the right place, whether you have goodwill or are filled with ill intent. That determines everything."

"Well, Dad, since you know that, shouldn't you try looking into your own heart?" she pounces, sounding more pointed than opposition questioning in parliament.

In any event, the heart is the source of a family's happiness, an individual's happiness and all happiness. The heart exists to produce infinite happiness. We must never allow such a deplorable realm of the heart to develop that it leads to parents and children harming or even killing one another.

Imagine a father, mother, son and daughter sharing inspiring quotes by various noted thinkers. There were the words of Homer, the ancient Greek poet, which Beethoven, in his bitter struggle against his destiny, had copied into his personal notebook, "The fates have given men enduring souls." This was the father's motto.

Next, they considered the words of Swiss philosopher Carl Hilty, "For [association] with persons whom one recognizes as bad demoralizes one's own nature." Here, the mother cautioned against getting involved with bad people or going out to seedy places.

The daughter read a quote from Rousseau, "Greatly did the pleasure of [knowledge's] acquisition contribute to my happiness."

She then turned to her father and said, "So, Dad, why don't we read the Daishonin's writings and study the guidance in SGI publications together?"

From Plato, "[Since] not one of us can escape our destiny [of inevitable death], we should then proceed to consider in what way we will best live out our allotted span of life."

"All of us will die one day," said the son. "That's why it's so important to create a life filled with good memories."

Everyone agreed. That is also why we are determined to fight on in our struggle. As Voltaire said: "Man is born for action. . . . Not to be doing anything is the same for man as not to exist."

The daughter then shared a statement by one of her favorite writers, China's Lu Xun: "The best part of being human is the opportunity to enjoy conversation and passionate discussion with many friends."

This led the son to say: "A friend recently sent me this quote from Mahatma Gandhi: 'I could not be leading a religious life unless I identified myself with the whole of humankind, and that I could not do unless I took part in politics. . . . You cannot divide social, economic, political and purely religious work into watertight compartments.'"

Finally, the father shared a quote from former French president and military general Charles de Gaulle: "Victory—there is no other option!"

Our fathers of *kosen-rufu* may be plain, ordinary men, but they are loved, and they are far more important than any member of parliament or government minister. They are great human beings, people of tremendous caliber. When one father pointed out a celebrity and a family that belonged to a leading business dynasty, his daughter proclaimed, "I think you're a hundred times better than any of those people."

Prestige and fame, titles and position have nothing to do with genuine happiness. Who is truly great? Those who strive the hardest and live the most earnestly. Those who follow their chosen path in life with the utmost dedication and commitment.

It's not a matter of your profession, how much money you have, how well known you are, your personal appearance or your social position. There are very famous politicians and celebrities who are ugly inside. People should be able to look up to their political leaders, but unfortunately, corrupt politicians betray the people's trust and commit monstrous injustices.

As sages of the past declared: "If the Law that one embraces is supreme, then the person who embraces it must accordingly be foremost among all others" (WND-1, 61). "Since the Law is wonderful, the person is worthy of respect; since the person is worthy of respect, the land is sacred" (WND-1, 1097).

Our ultimate greatness as human beings is determined by whether we uphold the supreme Buddhist teaching, the foremost philosophy and the highest ideals. Without a solid commitment to right principles, the human spirit remains empty and void of deep purpose. Unaware of the fundamental Law or truth governing all life, people seek only superficialities and cannot realize a world of genuine peace and happiness.

Policies and systems alone can never resolve the innumerable contradictions in human society. A spiritual solution is vital. That is why Nichiren Buddhism, which teaches the "great wisdom of equality" and the principle of "establishing the correct teaching for the peace of the land," is absolutely necessary.

Experiencing untold obstacles and hardships for the sake of the unsurpassed Law is the highest honor, and those who do so are great and worthy of respect above all.

The efforts of those in our Soka Gakkai men's groups for retired men sixty and older are remarkable. I heard about a seventy-two-year-old member who was inspired by their vigorous example. Having been invited to a meeting and thinking to take his prayer beads, he opened the drawer of his Buddhist altar for the first time in quite awhile. He found a piece of paper there, yellowed with age, and saw the familiar handwriting of his wife, who had died nearly a decade earlier. It was a prayer: "May my husband's asthma get better soon." Realizing how much she had been chanting for him, he resolved to make a sincere effort from that day onward to practice as hard as two people, doing her part as well. His fellow members all shared the joy of his fresh start. The triumph of the men is the triumph of the women, too.

The fathers of *kosen-rufu* have become lion kings. Their eyes shine with invincible courage and justice.

They have become champions of humanity, holding aloft the jeweled sword of truth, valiantly taking on and winning over every injustice and wrongdoing. Their ferocity in challenging all who would subvert justice and truth is the epitome of a lion king. And they have become fathers of committed faith, ready to face a thousand opponents in the struggle for truth.

Our fathers are strong! Our fathers are victorious!

(from the July 30, 2004, World Tribune, *p. 1)*

Men on the Great, Everlasting Path
Thoughts on 'The New Human Revolution'

As LONG AS I POSSESS a lofty philosophy, I can overcome all adversity. For the unparalleled drama of the human spirit lies in transforming adversity into profound happiness.

This is precisely where Buddhism comes in. I wish to pass on the torch of my spirit—its flame never diminishing, growing ever higher—to my comrades and future generations.

Whatever vexing conflicts I may encounter in life, whatever persecution motivated by vanity and jealousy is directed at me, even though I may be bloodied and battered, I am determined to attain proud victory.

My comrades, my fellow members! No matter what dire hardship may befall you, though you may be pierced through and through with arrows, do not be defeated. No matter what dastardly, cowardly attack is made on your morale, always remain proud and lead a noble life in the highest of spirits.

"Never a day without a line"—these are words of the ancient Roman writer Pliny the Elder. I am grateful that this essay series has continued for five years. I dedicate this essay to the golden pillars of *kosen-rufu,* the men of the SGI.

Life is filled with problems and difficulties. We never know what will happen next. There are constant challenges at work. There is the prospect of being laid off due to corporate restructuring, having one's company go bankrupt, becoming unemployed and having to find a new job. In our families and communities, too, problems are constantly pressing—sickness, issues with our children and our relationships with others.

On top of this, the crushing waves of a deep recession continue to batter the economy, with individuals, businesses and every sort of organization caught in a desperate struggle to survive.

I am also a member of the men's division. Though men usually don't talk about these things, I am keenly aware of the hardships facing you, my comrades in arms.

I recall how after the war, when I began to work for second Soka Gakkai president Josei Toda, we were in the midst of a period of dramatic change brought about by the economic policies during the U.S. occupation. It was a time of fierce, merciless competition in which only the strong survived.

Even President Toda, brilliant entrepreneur that he was, experienced business failures. Normally stalwart and imperturbable, he suffered so much that he awoke each morning in sheets soaked with perspiration from worrying through the night. As a youth, I devoted myself to my job with single-minded dedication, determined to serve and protect my mentor with all my being.

President Toda eventually rode out the worst and, rising like the sun, was inaugurated as second president when he was fifty-one.

The Japanese word for *man* suggests vigor. The true spirit of men in their prime is to look positively to the future.

American entrepreneur Dr. Armand Hammer, whom I met several times, once said that if we allow ourselves to be discouraged, we make ourselves our own worst enemy.

He also used to say: "If I had listened to all the people who have told me, 'It can't be done,' I would never have done anything. I always say, 'Don't tell me it can't be done: tell me *how* I can do it.'" Dr. Hammer burned with an indefatigable spirit of challenge.

In an address he gave at Soka University of Japan more than a decade ago, he reflected on his tumultuous life of ninety-two years, "If you stick to your original objective, you can as one individual change the situation."

When Shijo Kingo, the illustrious predecessor of the SGI men, was ordered by his lord to abandon the Lotus Sutra or risk losing his lands, Nichiren Daishonin offered him stern guidance. He said that if Shijo Kingo were to give in, his opponents would induce all the Daishonin's followers in Kamakura to abandon faith. Do not be defeated, he urged. The pillar must not fall.

The Daishonin writes: "This life is like a dream. One cannot be sure that one will live until tomorrow. However wretched a beggar you might become, never disgrace the Lotus Sutra" (WND-1, 824).

Shijo Kingo courageously persevered through this trial. Acting with sincerity and integrity, based on the Daishonin's admonition that our behavior as human beings is the ultimate expression of faith, he summoned all his wisdom to overcome this hurdle.

He conducted himself modestly and was considerate and attentive to all around him. He emerged from this painful period of tribulation as a victor, praised by all as "Shijo Kingo, Shijo Kingo of the Lotus school," just as the Daishonin had hoped (WND-1, 319).

Buddhism is about emerging triumphant.

The men of the SGI are the pillars of the family and society; they are the great golden pillars of *kosen-rufu*. Precisely because the men are strong and resolute, the women and youth can engage in their challenges with confidence and peace of mind.

The ancient Greek poet Sophocles wrote: "And for men, to help [others] / With might and main is of all tasks the highest."

In your hearts shine medals of supreme, eternal honor. You have triumphed. You have not been beaten. A lofty life is beautiful.

Those who live their lives with such true beauty are victors. The essence of this beauty is our inner determination, in accord with the principle of a single moment of life encompassing three thousand realms; it is our spirit, our mind that matters.

Life is a series of labyrinths. But, my friends, strive for the noble goal you have pledged to realize. Do not get sidetracked and lose your way.

In our world today, many lead lives of despair. Society is full of suffering and rampant with causes leading to tragic destruction. There are those who only close themselves off further as they struggle painfully through life. There are those who go to their grave in bleak misery, weeping tears of regret at their own foolishness, and there are vain pretenders who close their eyes, heavy with remorse as they depart this life.

Life is long.

No, life is all too brief.

My friends, drink a toast to victory while enjoying the sunshine. Drink a toast to glory while watching shooting stars streak across the night sky. And sing the song of your vow in resounding voices, solemn and strong, while gazing up at the moon, savoring life's incandescent happiness.

Self-pity, defeat and tears are not for us. We will win in our struggle. Never allow fools, cowards or traitors to encroach!

With a gaze radiating compassion and understanding, with bright smiles and pleasant voices, let us live out our lives encouraging our family members and comrades in faith. When I meet you, I am filled with joy. Walking with you is to walk a noble path.

We embrace a solid mission in life. Envy-inspired furors are of no concern to us.

There are people who may enjoy enthusiastic applause now. There are others who may be feted by the media. There are also pitiful individuals who are prisoners of their own rapacious, gem-hungry egos. And there are those who, tragically, are heading for a precipitous fall.

The banner of hollow fame and pretension is bound to become ragged and tattered. Fame is not happiness. It is not true victory.

And those who circulate false rumors in an attempt to cause others' downfall are destined to end their foolish lives as objects of scorn and ridicule.

We, on the other hand, walk the great, everlasting path of life with confidence and integrity. Forging a brilliant realm of indestructible happiness in our hearts and dreams, we advance youthfully, meaningfully and resolutely day after day.

Along this path, flowers bloom and perfume the air. We spend each day of our existence savoring the joy of life caressed by a refreshing, laurel-scented breeze.

My friends, boldly extend your broad wings, draw the sword of truth and justice, and fight and triumph!

Life is a struggle. Truth and justice must win in that struggle.

My friends, do not content yourselves with walking a mundane, easy road. Fight for your freedom and glory with pride and determination. Do not become hypocrites or frauds. Do not lead gray, withered lives of remorse.

Rouse yourselves and struggle courageously for what is right. As long as you live, dare to challenge and triumph over every storm, every raging wave.

My friends, who possess a spirit of indomitable determination, who shine with pride, happiness and integrity as emperors of life! Write a new page of history with every challenge, as part of your noble mission to achieve victory.

My friends, do not create a path of defeat and tragedy. Build a great path of happiness and triumph.

My friends, you see it! You see the spread of Nichiren Buddhism across the world, a development as certain as the sun's daily ascent, unfailing and eternal.

The law of this great path, assuring certain eternal victory, towers in your lives. On the road ahead, there is no anxiety, no defeat, no retreat and indeed no end. There are truth, justice, freedom and the golden, joyous cries of the people.

There is no regret, no anger—only a song of eternal happiness. We have triumphed. Indeed, we must continue to do so. We must eternally advance in victory.

We have said farewell forever to that nightmarish time when we were ridiculed and wept aloud. The spring breeze embraces us. The stars, those everlasting medals of honor, gaze down upon us.

Your struggle and the earnest, dedicated spirit with which you have won over all, have forged deeply inspiring lives that will shine and live forever. Your victory is not a distinction stained by bloodshed. It is not a distinction gained through the agonies of a vile conflict between human beings. It is not an ostentatious distinction awarded by arrogant authority. It is the culmination of all your efforts to ensure that truth and justice prevail. The ramparts of your life will never crumble.

There are no greater kings of happiness than those who possess the boundless, immeasurable wealth of "many treasures"—the life-state of Buddhahood—which is more precious than any reward or medal of honor.

My friends, never forget these words of the Russian thinker Nikolai Berdyaev, who echoes our philosophy of human revolution, "The true revolution of the spirit is what interests me most." In his seventies, he also exclaimed: "My spirit never ages. My spirit is forever young."

(from the April 18, 2003, World Tribune, *p. 2, and the August 2003* Living Buddhism, *p. 5)*

Directing Our Lives Toward Health

August 24, 2002

To MY GREAT FRIENDS of the SGI-USA men's division, my sincere congratulations on your general meetings and conferences commemorating Aug. 24, SGI Men's Day! I understand that you are holding meaningful gatherings throughout this month on the theme of health. Thank you very much for all your efforts and hard work.

A healthy life is an earnest wish of all. Today may well be called an age of health, in which health has become a focus of people's concerns. Our SGI activities constitute a supreme way to health. Attending SGI meetings, visiting and encouraging our friends, engaging others in dialogue about Buddhism with our earnest desire for their happiness and for peace—these unceasing efforts in faith, practice and study are helping us build supremely healthy bodies and minds.

In the long course of our lives, we may fall ill at times. Nichiren Daishonin, however, encourages us, "Illness gives rise to the resolve to attain the way" (WND-1, 937). As the Daishonin says, no matter what may happen, it is Buddhism that enables us to change poison into medicine. If you have a friend suffering from illness, please do your best to encourage that person, for encouragement has the great power to direct people's lives toward health.

It is also our mission to build a healthy society. Your efforts to build solidarity based on the highest good, while increasing your brilliance and influence, will lead to the creation of a healthy society.

Each of you, please be convinced of your profound mission and live a great life of victory based on our magnificent faith.

Let me close my message with a prayer for the excellent health and ever-greater happiness of my treasured friends of the men's division and for the further development of the SGI-USA.

Daisaku Ikeda, SGI president

The Power of Courage

MARCH 9–12, 2000

On the occasion of the Men's Division Conference at the SGI-USA Florida Nature and Culture Center.

TO THE MEN'S DIVISION MEMBERS, who are great trees of *kosen-rufu*: My heartfelt congratulations on your conference! I truly appreciate your daily efforts for *kosen-rufu*. I am convinced that Nichiren Daishonin has been watching your steady, assiduous and respectable devotion to your communities throughout American society.

In "Letter from Sado," the Daishonin states, "Those with the heart of a lion king are sure to attain Buddhahood" (WND-1, 302). A cowardly mind can do nothing to help the sun of hope arise from within, nor can it raise the curtain on a new stage.

Always, it is the power of one's courage that opens the way ahead. Faith is another name for the utmost courage. Once a man stands up, *kosen-rufu* in his environment will greatly progress. Those who now brace their courage and fight for *kosen-rufu* and justice with the spirit of a lion king will surely enjoy ever-greater vitality. They will obtain a life-condition as free as the Buddha's.

Please take leadership majestically and dauntlessly. Live the greatest life, powerfully, together with me. You all are important to me. I pray for your good health and happiness. I also pray for the good health and happiness of your family members and friends. Please stay in good health and high spirits forever.

DAISAKU IKEDA, SGI PRESIDENT

Your Noble Voyage of Life

—Dedicated to my most respected and esteemed men's division members

He was a nameless elementary school principal;
He was unknown, yet a master geographer;
He was a hero of *kosen-rufu*,
Who practiced as the Buddha taught.

And he was the founder
Of the Soka Gakkai
With its tradition of *shakubuku*,
The practice of the Lotus Sutra.

He died a martyr to his beliefs
As a towering practitioner of the Mystic Law,
The ultimate law of life
Revealed by Nichiren Daishonin.

In 1928,
At the age of fifty-seven,
Our great predecessor Tsunesaburo Makiguchi
Began his selfless struggle to propagate the Law.
Later speaking of his jubilation, he said to his disciples,
"With an inexpressible sense of joy,
I transformed the way I lived my life for almost sixty years!"

At the age of fifty-nine,
Our first president, Mr. Makiguchi,
Founded the Soka Kyoiku Gakkai—
Society for Value-creating Education.

He stood as firm as a rock,
Defeating countless onslaughts
In his battle against the treacherous authorities
And in his struggle against base, evil priests
Who looked down on ordinary people.
He advanced with powerful conviction,
Giving his crimson lifeblood to the struggle.

At times,
His family and followers
Looked at their noble father beseechingly,
Fearful of possible persecution.

At times
His followers paled at the sight
Of their stern father
Clad in the armor of indescribable suffering.

In his path lay the obstructions of autocratic authorities;
In his path loomed persecutions by the military.
Yet he refused to retreat,
Boldly advancing instead as a lion,
Pressing forward, ever forward.

Many of his disciples wandered lost
In a desert wasteland.
But he alone,
The lion championing lofty beliefs,

Crossing valley after valley,
His glinting gaze focused on the future,
Never ceased in his quest.

In prison,
Having kept his fight for justice alive
Until the final moment of his life,
Having faithfully upheld the banner of peace
And left the mark of his struggle forever in history,
Mr. Makiguchi died
At the age of seventy-three,
Giving his life for his beliefs.

The membership of three thousand
That had followed him
Had been crushed and cast asunder
By the unrelenting religious persecution of the military.
But Mr. Makiguchi's peerless disciple, Josei Toda,
Whose heart was at one with his own—
A disciple serving his true and eternal mentor—
Shook with rage and wept bitter tears
In his own dark, cramped prison cell,
The news of his mentor's passing
Sending him almost mad with grief.

Driven by sorrow, pain, anger
And a burning desire for vengeance,
Josei Toda began a spiritual odyssey,
Determined to triumph proudly without fail
Over the evil powers
That had caused his beloved mentor,
A great champion of justice,
To die in prison.

Josei Toda was eventually released from prison,
Carrying within him a monumental state of being.
He began an eternal movement to rectify
The insidious and violent abuses of authoritarian power.
It was the bold, new start
Of a war on falsehood and arrogance.

His tireless efforts
Ignited a flame from heart to heart
And comprised a continuous struggle,
Leaving his disciples with his will and testament
To carry on his work if he should fall.
He lived each moment of this precious existence
As if it were his last,
Continuing to fight with the indomitable force
Of a charging lion.

It is already more than forty years
Since the great Josei Toda
Passed from our midst
Like the ebbing tide.
Convinced of life's eternity,
We comrades of like mind who were his disciples
Resolved to carry on his work without fail.
I, as befitting a direct disciple,
Stood in the vanguard amid the gathering storm,
Many disciples in turn following my lead.

Both first president Makiguchi
And my mentor, President Toda,
Would have been members
Of what is today
Our proud men's division.

They had no crown, no fame.
Enduring criticism and abuse,
They pressed on
From one struggle of the Law to another,
In complete accord with the teachings of Nichiren Daishonin.

My mentor Josei Toda
Often used to say:
"Let cowards depart!
Let deserters leave!
Let critics say what they will!"

The burning entity of our beings
Is directly linked to the Daishonin
And to the spirit of *kosen-rufu*.

We have tears of compassion
And the strength of the noonday sun.
In dark times of hardship, too,
We have beautiful and noble hearts.
We are embraced in the greatest treasure of the universe,
Faith.

Both Mr. Makiguchi and Mr. Toda cried out:
"Come, come and join us, heroic youth!
Youth who will advance intrepidly into the storm!
Disciples who will not weep at approaching persecution,
But who will fight on with composure!
Youth who will continue the glorious advance
To the infinite ends of the earth!"

No one can help but be awed by
The solemn life-to-life bond

Of mentor and disciple,
The highest of all human bonds.
Traitors will suffer inevitable defeat and disappear;
Cowards will unquestionably incur negative effects.

Celebrating with magnificent music,
The heavenly deities throughout three existences
Will protect this noble march of mentor and disciple.
Those who are jealous of, and who criticize and attack,
Our procession of *kosen-rufu*, of mentor and disciple,
Are of zero significance.

Joyous is our song of glory!
Exuberant is the music that fills our life!
We walk in this garden of our eternal destiny—
How admirable is our way of life!

The hearts of all who do so
Enjoy the heavens' eternal felicitations
Which encompass all things—
Stars, moon, forests and clouds.
This path is true!
It is the path of the self's true mission—
A path without regrets!

Poet and fighter Victor Hugo sang,
"Life is a voyage!"
Proclaiming himself an invincible lion,
He kept moving forward vigorously, without ceasing,
Pushing back the angry, surging waves
That threatened to engulf him.

He lived a regal drama,
Surmounting all persecutions
And plots of exile.
He cried:
"Thunder, roar as you will!
For I'll roar back even louder!"

Chinese Premier Zhou Enlai,
Who dedicated his life to revolution
And to the construction of a new China,
Maintained,
"Victory cannot be achieved
By sitting and waiting for it to happen;
It must be won through struggle."
His heart remained ever youthful
Regardless of his advancing years.
He always stood at the head of the struggle,
Becoming the driving force for victory.

We who are advancing *kosen-rufu*,
The noblest of all humanity's endeavors,
Must never be afraid!
Must never be defeated!

If we cease in our efforts,
The Daishonin would sorrow
And humankind would be destroyed by barbarism.
We would fall under the pall of eternal darkness,
Set adrift amid interminable suffering
And an unending cycle of misery.

Nichiren Daishonin writes:
"Now Nichiren and his followers

Who invoke Nam-myoho-renge-kyo
Are like a great wind blowing."
"Nam-myoho-renge-kyo is like the roar of a lion."
What supremely confident words these are!

The fainthearted may despair,
The weak-willed may flee,
But we will write a noble history of life,
Day after day, year after year,
Our hearts—yours and mine—burning ever brightly,
As we pursue the journey of life across eternity,
Laughing aloud at the world's frenzied criticisms,
Seeing, appreciating and extolling
All that is most beautiful in this world,
In this age of the Latter Day of the Law,
Which is ruled by a dark destiny.

Sharing heart-to-heart ties
With so many precious, treasured friends,
How joyful and boisterous will be our lives,
Even after death and across the three existences!
What an exquisite and indestructible
Achievement of honor it is
To share this voyage of life with comrades,
Together celebrating our victory,
Bathed in the moon's beautiful light!

How sad and vain are the lives
Of those left behind.
The Daishonin writes,
"The thoughtless are no more than animals."
Do not become alienated from the harmonious community
Of believers dedicated to *kosen-rufu*

And fall into the hell of loneliness!
Solitude may seem free of constraints,
But it is like a shattered spirit
That has lost its center.

Nichiren Daishonin writes,
"Buddhism primarily concerns itself
With victory or defeat."
The Daishonin's great persecutions
For the sake of Buddhism
All arose as a result of false accusations!
The human heart can be frightening, sinister and dark.
The persecution of followers like Shijo Kingo
Was also the work of treacherous colleagues.

Why did the priesthood decline?
Because of its arrogance and envy!
Because of its laziness and negligence!
Because of its idleness and chatter!
Because of its smugness and conceit!
Because of its greed and ignorance!
Because of its slander and lies!
Because of its destroying the harmonious unity of believers!

Why did the Gakkai develop?
Because of our selfless dedication!
Because of our unceasing devotion!
Because of our treasuring the Law more highly than our own lives!
Because of our brave and diligent exertion!
Because of our perseverance and fortitude!
Because of our spirit of oneness of mentor and disciple!
Because of our unity of *itai doshin*—many in body, one in mind!

My friends in the men's division,
It is vital that you win in society
And in the workplace,
That you form bonds of trust and friendship with many others,
That you be a citadel that provides a happy haven for your family,
And that, with vigorous good health,
You triumph in the arduous struggles of daily life!

Your life, your being,
Is yours for all time—past, present and future.
Thus everything depends on
How you forge yourself,
How you improve yourself,
How you live a happy life—
This is the aim of human revolution.

Buddhism expounds the law of cause and effect,
Enabling us to transform our lives throughout eternity.
Buddhism keenly elucidates
The essence of this causal law of life.
This law is strict, it says,
Operating across the three thousand realms
In a single moment of life.
Buddhism surpasses all other philosophies
In clarifying the fundamental reality of life.

The Law does not exist outside our own lives.
The law of cause and effect
Is the reality of all phenomena in the universe.
Cause and effect exist simultaneously!
We are swept along by the inexorable flow of time
That comprises causes and effects in each moment.

We must know
That there is a profound connection
Between good and evil,
Happiness and unhappiness,
Hell and Buddhahood.

My dear friends, my comrades!
May you strive for good health and longevity!
For that is the first step to happiness and victory.

Be big-hearted!
Be deep-hearted!
Be warm-hearted!
Be strong-hearted!
There you will find the banner of victory
Of Buddhist practice.

Wherever you go,
Be a pillar of strength who brings peace of mind to all!
Be a person of magnanimous character who inspires hope!

Become a champion of humanism
Who makes the place where you are now
Shine as the Treasure Tower!

March 26, 1999

Daisaku Ikeda
World Poet Laureate

The True Way To Live With Dignity as Men

AUGUST 20, 1999

On the occasion of the Men's Division Conferences, held the last two weekends of August at the Florida Nature and Culture Center, commemorating August 24, Men's Division Day.

I WANT TO EXPRESS my appreciation and congratulations for the great efforts you have made in attending these conferences for the SGI-USA men's division members, whom I deeply respect.

As a member of the men's division myself, please allow me to send my congratulations.

Shijo Kingo is considered one of the greatest predecessors of the men's division. Nichiren Daishonin says to him, "It is better to live a single day with honor than to live to 120 and die in disgrace" (WND-1, 851).

I firmly believe that as men's division members, we should create a solid history of faith by living to the fullest for the sake of *kosen-rufu*. This is the treasure of the heart, the greatest human value. In faith, in character, in society—in every realm of our lives—let's climb the slope of growth and development without taking a single step back. This is the true way to live with dignity as men.

I earnestly hope that all of you, the SGI-USA men's division members, advance refreshed, making each moment a new start. Aim to be victors in life and victors in faith, with the spirit of eternal youth. And never forget to respect women and warmly embrace youth.

I pray that all of you enjoy good health and prosperity and that your families be endowed with boundless good fortune. Please convey my best regards to the men's division members in every district of the SGI-USA.

DAISAKU IKEDA, SGI PRESIDENT

Our Time Has Come

MANY MEMBERS PLACE GREAT TRUST and expectation in the men's division members, the pillars of *kosen-rufu*. The women's division members, the compassionate mothers of *kosen-rufu*, are never shy about voicing those expectations.

"Why aren't the men more enthusiastic?" they ask. I say that the men's division members *are* enthusiastic; they just don't make a show of it. They want to surprise everyone in the end with a brilliant achievement—like the quiet man who turns out to be a hero at the climax of a great drama.

Others ask, "Why are they so reluctant to act?" I say that the men *aren't* reluctant; they are prudent. They don't want to waste their efforts. They know the importance of waiting until the time is ripe.

"Why are they so timid?" asks another. "Why don't they speak up?" I say that they're *not* timid; they're just thoughtful. They choose their words carefully, out of consideration for others and to avoid meaningless babble.

I am also a men's division member, and I am quite aware of the feelings and circumstances of my beloved fellow members.

Many of the men's division members are facing incredible challenges. Thinking of their families' happiness, they boldly brave the winds of economic recession, racking their brains and working twice as hard as others to excel at work. For the most part, however, their wives and children don't get the chance to witness this side of them. And when, on one of their rare days off, our men's division members want to rest peacefully at home, they are criticized for "just sitting around all day, doing nothing."

Those who are fathers, meanwhile, find themselves shunned and scorned once their adored children hit adolescence. Whenever the budget is tight, Dad's spending money is always the first to be cut. If he complains, his wife will fire back: "Why don't you quit smoking and cut down on your drinking? It'll be good for your health, too."

There are times when even a reasonable argument just adds to one's already heavy pressures.

Yet even under these trying circumstances, how wonderful it is to see the men striving hard in Soka Gakkai activities, devoting themselves for the sake of Buddhism, society and their fellow members.

The Japanese word for *men* suggests vigor. Nichiren Daishonin was fifty when he faced the persecution at Tatsunokuchi and revealed his true identity as the original Buddha. And Shijo Kingo, who stood up to defend him and accompanied him at that time of crisis, had just turned forty.

It was thus in his forties that Shijo Kingo traveled all the way to visit and seek guidance from the Daishonin at his place of exile, Sado Island. Shijo Kingo went on to prove the justice and power of Buddhism despite the adverse circumstances of having his fief confiscated. In this sense, we may say that Shijo Kingo was a pioneering member of the men's division rather than the youth division.

Centuries later, Tsunesaburo Makiguchi embraced the Daishonin's teachings at age fifty-seven. His intellectual and philosophical search led him finally to the Daishonin's Buddhism, and from there his journey of *kosen-rufu* began. Furthermore, Josei Toda was forty-five when, in prison, he realized that it was his mission to make the widespread propagation of the Daishonin's teachings a reality.

In his novel *The Human Revolution* (written under the pen name Myo Goku), Mr. Toda shows through the main character, Gan, how to reveal one's true potential. In one scene, Gan has awakened to faith in the Daishonin's Buddhism and is showing actual proof of that faith at work:

> How strong a person can become through a simple change in attitude! You can either tell yourself, "It's too hard, I don't think I'll be able to do it," or "Yes, I can do this. Let me at it." Only a fine line separates the two. But I'll tell you one thing, if you work like crazy, you'll come to display capabilities that you never had before—or rather, I should say, capabilities or potential that you always possessed but never before tapped.

Dynamic growth begins with a positive determination. And unflagging effort is the key to breaking through our limitations. Faith is a never-ending process of challenging ourselves.

The men's division members are the cornerstones of the Soka Gakkai. They are the last runners in the relay race of *kosen-rufu*, the runners who determine our victory or defeat.

The men's division members are lions. Their indomitable presence gives assurance to those around them. When their resolute voices ring out, they instill courage in everyone and bring about a victory of the people.

My heroic friends! My noble comrades in the struggle for *kosen-rufu*! A decisive battle to usher in the dawn of the twenty-first century has already begun. At last, our time has come.

If we do not rise to the challenge now, then when? If we do not fight today, then when?

Life is a struggle against the limited time we have on earth.

What will have been the purpose of our lives if we do not fulfill our mission? If we abandon our dream, no matter how we may try to justify ourselves, there will be little left in the end but emptiness and regret.

The Daishonin writes, "You must not spend your lives in vain and regret it for ten thousand years to come" (WND-1, 622). Let us leap astride our white horses and gallop intrepidly across the great plains of our mission, holding high the banner of *kosen-rufu*.

(from the July 10, 1998, World Tribune, *p. 4)*